Time and Money

From the Read-Aloud Anthology

MY BIG NIGHT

by Harold Mitchell

illustrated by Josée Masse

Access Prior Knowledge
This story will help you review
- Addition and subtraction facts through 10
- Order

Tonight at **7** o'clock
I'll be acting in a play.

But it's only _____ o'clock.
It's still **6** hours away.

Tonight at **7** o'clock
I'll be roaring in a play.

But it's only _____ o'clock.
It's still **2** hours away.

Name _____

Use the number line.
Write the number.

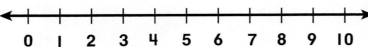

0 1 2 3 4 5 6 7 8 9 10

1. The family eats dinner at 5 o'clock. Which number is just after 5? _____

2. The play starts at 7 o'clock. Which number is just before 7? _____

1

2

3

3. What does the girl in the story do before the play?

_____

4. What does she do after dinner?

_____

5. **Talk About It** What do you do before and after dinner?

Dear Family,

My class is starting Unit 5. I will be learning about time, calendars, and counting money. These two pages show what I will learn and have activities for us to do together.

From, _____

Vocabulary

These are some words I will use in this unit.

hour hand The shorter hand on a clock

minute hand The longer hand on a clock

minute hand → hour hand

digital A type of clock that does not have a minute hand or an hour hand

calendar A chart that shows days, weeks, and months

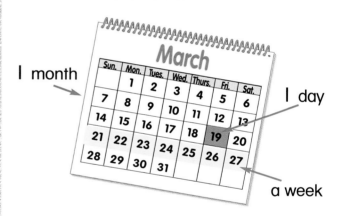

I month

I day

a week

Some other words I will use are **minute**, **hour**, **penny**, **nickel**, **dime**, and **quarter**.

Vocabulary Activity

Let's work together to complete these sentences.

Turn the page for more.

1. The shorter hand on a clock is the _____,

   and the longer hand is the _____.

2. A _____ shows days, weeks, and months.

3. A _____ clock does not have a minute hand or an hour hand.

HOW TO understand time

I will be learning how to tell time on different clocks.
Sometimes I will use a clock to show minutes and hours.

minute	hour
A minute has 60 seconds. Some activities take about 1 minute.	An hour has 60 minutes. Some activities take about 1 hour.
Tying your shoe can take about 1 minute.	Playing a game can take about 1 hour.

Draw what you can do in about 1 minute.

Draw what you can do in about 1 hour.

◆ Literature

These books link to the math in this unit.
We can look for them at the library.

How Long?
By Elizabeth Dale
Illustrated by Alan Marks
(Orchard Books, 1998)

The Purse
By Kathy Caple

Let's read together!

What Time Is It, Mr. Wolf?
By Bob Beeson

Education Place

We can visit *Education Place* at

eduplace.com/maf

for the Math Lingo game,
*e•*Glossary, and more games
and activities to do together.

Time and Calendar

INVESTIGATION

Find the clocks in the shop that are not working right and tell why.

Before and After School

Draw something you do in the morning before school.

These kids are busy learning at school during the day.

Draw something you do in the evening.

Name_____

Order Events

Some events happen **before** others.
Some events happen **after** others.
Many events happen in order.

Objective
Put events in order.

Vocabulary
before
after

Guided Practice

Write 1, 2, and 3 to show the correct order.

Think
First, the girl gets the box of blocks.

1.

2.

Explain Your Thinking What do you do before lunch at school? What do you do after lunch?

Remember to think about which event happens first.

Write 1, 2, and 3 to show the correct order.

1.

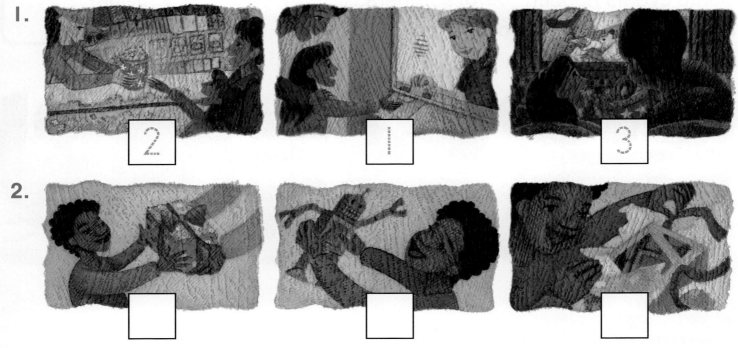

2.

Draw three pictures in order to show things you did today.

3.

| 1 | 2 | 3 |

Problem Solving ▶ Reasoning

Mato brushes his teeth.
Next he reads a story.
Then he goes to bed.

4. What does Mato do before he reads a story?

_____

5. What does Mato do after he reads a story?

_____

At Home Discuss your child's daily routine. Have your child use the words **before** and **after** to tell about the events.

Activity: Estimate a Minute

If you know how long a **minute** is, you can find out what takes more or less than 1 minute.

Objective
Compare time.
Vocabulary
minute

Hands-On

about 1 minute

more than 1 minute

Work Together

Step 1

Think about how long it takes to write the numbers 1 to 50.

about 1 minute

more than 1 minute

less than 1 minute

Step 2

Try it.
Start writing the numbers.
Your teacher will tell you when 1 minute has passed.

In 1 minute I wrote the numbers 1 to _____.

Try activities you are
not sure about.

Circle the activity if it takes about I minute.
Draw an X on the activity if it takes more than I minute.

1.

2.

3.

4.

5.

6.

7. **Write About It** How do you know if an activity takes
more than I minute?

_____

_____

Look at the projects.

A

B

C

8. What project takes the longest time to make? _____

9. What project takes the shortest time to make? _____

At Home Name activities and discuss with your child which ones you can do in about
I minute. Then discuss activities that are shorter and longer than I minute.

Hour

The **hour hand** and the **minute hand** show the time on some clocks.

Digital clocks show the time using only numbers.

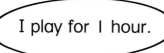

I play for 1 hour.

The minute hand is at the 12.

The hour hand is at the 4.

The game starts at 4 **o'clock.**

I **hour** later is 5 o'clock

Guided Practice

Read the clock.
Write the time two ways.

Think
The shorter hand is the hour hand.

1.

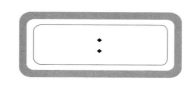

_____ o'clock

2.

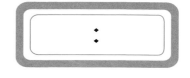

_____ o'clock

Explain Your Thinking Where do the hands point on a clock showing 7 o'clock?

Practice

Read the clock.
Write the time two ways.

Remember the shorter hand is the hour hand.

1.

5:00

__5__ o'clock

2.

:

_____ o'clock

3.

:

_____ o'clock

4.

:

_____ o'clock

5.

:

_____ o'clock

6.

:

_____ o'clock

Problem Solving ▸ Data Sense

Mia eats dinner at 6:00.

7. Ken eats dinner later than Mia.
   What time does he eat?   _____

8. How many children eat earlier
   than Mia?

   _____ children

Dinner Times

Number of Children

6
5
4
3
2
1
0

5:00 6:00 7:00
Time

364 three hundred sixty-four

At Home Have your child practice telling time to the hour. Use a variety of clocks.

Half-Hour

 Audio Tutor 2 / I Listen and Understand

An hour has **60** minutes.

A **half-hour** has **30** minutes.

The hour hand is halfway between the 8 and the 9.

The minute hand has gone halfway around the clock. It is at the 6.

8 o'clock

 minutes after   or half past __8__

Guided Practice

Say and write the time.

1.

_____ o'clock   half past _____

2.

 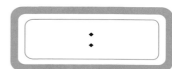

half past _____   _____ o'clock

Explain Your Thinking If the hour hand is halfway between the **4** and the **5**, and the minute hand is at the **6**, what time is it? Tell the time in two ways.

Practice

Say and write the time.

Remember when it is 30 minutes after the hour, the minute hand is at the 6.

1.

11:00

11:30

_____ o'clock   half past _____

2.

[:]   [:]

half past _____   _____ o'clock

3.

[:]   [:]

_____ o'clock   half past _____

Go on

366 three hundred sixty-six

Say and write the time.

4.

half past _____   _____ o'clock

5.

_____ o'clock   half past _____

Problem Solving ▶ Patterns

Write the time the clock shows.

6.

____:____   ____:____   ____:____   ____:____

7. Talk About It Explain the pattern you see above.

Now Try This   **Five Minutes**

Use what you know about counting by 5s to tell time to five minutes.

2:20

20 minutes after 2

Write the time.

1.

3:05

> **Think**
> It takes the minute hand 5 minutes to move from the 12 to the 1.

2.

___:___

3.

___:___

4.

___:___

5.

___:___

6.

___:___

7.

___:___

8.

___:___

Name_____

Elapsed Time

Objective
Find elapsed time.

Hands-On

A clock can help you find how long an activity takes.

Start

4:30

I practice for 1 hour.

End

5:30

Guided Practice

Use a clock.

Write how long the activity takes.

1. **Start**

Think
Move the hands 2 hours later.

End

_____ hours

2. **Start**

End

_____ hour

Draw the time the activity ends.

3. **Start**

I hour swimming

End

Explain Your Thinking Name an activity that takes about I hour.

It takes 60 minutes for the hands to move 1 hour around the clock.

Use a clock.
Write how long the activity takes.

1. Start | End

9:00 **12:00**

___3___ hours

2. Start | End

3:30 **5:30**

_____ hours

3. Start | End

_____ hours

4. Start | End

_____ hours

5. Start | End

12:00 **1:00**

_____ hour

6. Start | End

8:30 **11:30**

_____ hours

7. Start | End

_____ hours

8. Start | End

_____ hour

Go on

Name ______________________ **Practice**

Use a clock.
Show when the activity starts or ends.

	Start	Activity	End
9.		 1 hour finding shells	
10.	__ : __	 2 hours on the boat	4:00
11.		 3 hours building a sand castle	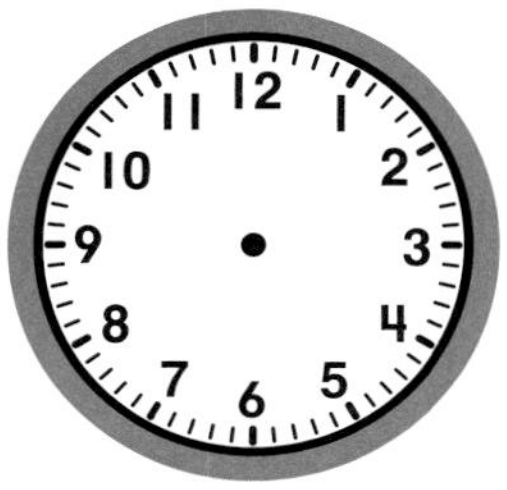
12.	6:30	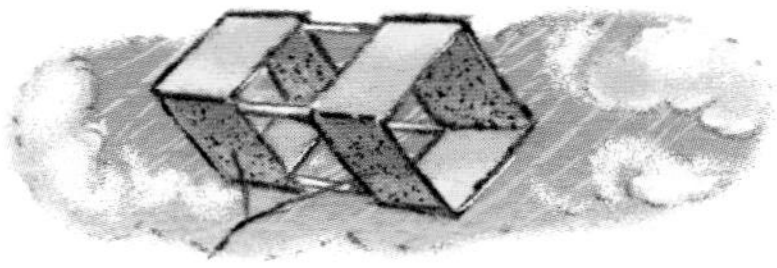 1 hour flying a kite	__ : __

Problem Solving ▶ Reasoning

The clocks show when the children eat lunch.

12:00	12:30	11:30
Ana	Patrice	Tyler

13. Who eats lunch earlier than Ana? ______________

At Home Discuss with your child when daily activities start and end. Help your child find out how long each activity takes.

Write 1, 2, and 3 to show the correct order.

1.

Circle the activity if it takes about **1** minute.
Draw an X on the activity if it takes more than **1** minute.

2.

Read the clock.
Write the time two ways.

Write how long the activity takes.

3.

_____ o'clock

4. **Start**   **End**

_____ hours

Write the time.

5.

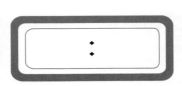

_____ o'clock

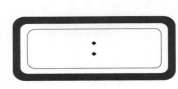

half past _____

Facts Practice, see page 675

Practice Telling Time

The same time can be shown in different ways.

Guided Practice

Show the time on the two clocks.

1. **8** o'clock

2. half past **1**

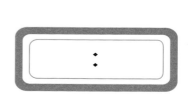

3. **11** o'clock

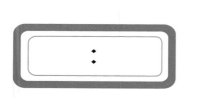

4. half past **5**

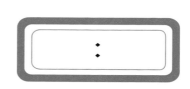

Explain Your Thinking Why is it important to be able to tell time on different kinds of clocks?

Practice

The short hand on a clock shows the hour.

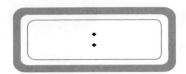
The first number on a digital clock shows the hour.

Show the time on the clock.

1. School starts at half past 8.

2. Math class starts at 9 o'clock.

3. We read a story at half past 10.

4. We play at half past 11.

5. Lunch time is at 12 o'clock.

6. School is over at half past 3.

Problem Solving ▶ Reasoning

7. Look at the pairs of clocks.

If they show the same time write S.
If they show different times write D.

_____ _____

At Home Help your child find and read signs that tell when stores, libraries, and other places open.

Name_____

Days and Weeks

 Audio Tutor 2/3 Listen and Understand

A **calendar** shows the months, weeks, and days of a year.

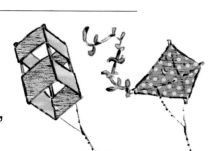

March

Sunday	Monday	Tuesday	Wednesday	Thursday	Friday	Saturday
	1	2	3	4	5	6
7	8	9	10	11	12	13
14	15	16	17	18	19	20
21	22	23	24	25	26	27
28	29	30	31			

Guided Practice

Use the calendar to find the answer.

Think
Count the days of the week from Sunday through Saturday.

1. How many days are in one week? _____

2. The name of the month is _____.

3. If today is Monday, what day will tomorrow be? _____

4. What is the day before Friday, March 26? _____

5. If yesterday was March 27, what is today's date? _____

Explain Your Thinking How can you tell if there are more Tuesdays or Fridays in the month shown above?

Fill in the calendar for this month.

The first date of the month can be any day of the week.

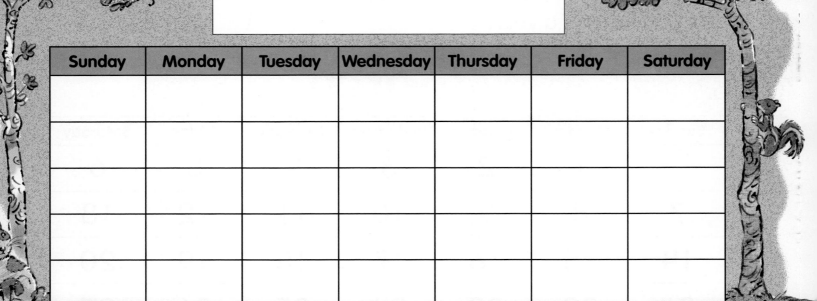

Sunday	Monday	Tuesday	Wednesday	Thursday	Friday	Saturday

Use the calendar to find the answer.

1. Color today ▭▬▶ .

2. Color yesterday ▭▬▶ .

3. Color tomorrow ▭▬▶ .

4. Color the first Sunday ▭▬▶ .

5. What day of the week is the ninth? _____

6. What is the date of the second Thursday in this month? _____

7. If today is the eleventh, what day of the week will tomorrow be? _____

Problem Solving ▶ Reasoning

8. What day of the week comes after the last date on your calendar? _____

9. What is the date of that day? _____

At Home Ask your child to read the dates of the Wednesdays shown on the calendar.

Months

There are 12 months in one year.

April

Here are the months of the year in order.

Sunday	Monday	Tuesday	Wednesday	Thursday	Friday	Saturday	
		1	2	3	4	5	January
6	7	8	9	10	11	12	February / March / April
13	14	15	16	17	18	19	May / June / July
20	21	22	23	24	25	26	August / September / October
27	28	29	30				November / December

Guided Practice

Use the calendar and list of months. Find the answer.

Think
The first day of this month is a Tuesday. Then there are 4 more.

1. How many Tuesdays are in this month? _____

2. What is the twelfth month of the year? _____

3. What month comes before June? _____

4. How many months come after April? _____

Explain Your Thinking What months come between August and December?

Use the calendars to find the answer.

May

Sun.	Mon.	Tues.	Wed.	Thurs.	Fri.	Sat.
				1	2	3
4	5	6	7	8	9	10
11	12	13	14	15	16	17
18	19	20	21	22	23	24
25	26	27	28	29	30	31

June

Sun.	Mon.	Tues.	Wed.	Thurs.	Fri.	Sat.
1	2	3	4	5	6	7
8	9	10	11	12	13	14
15	16	17	18	19	20	21
22	23	24	25	26	27	28
29	30					

July

Sun.	Mon.	Tues.	Wed.	Thurs.	Fri.	Sat.
		1	2	3	4	5
6	7	8	9	10	11	12
13	14	15	16	17	18	19
20	21	22	23	24	25	26
27	28	29	30	31		

1. Which of these months has the fewest days? _____ June _____

2. Which month has 5 Wednesdays? _____

3. Cinco de Mayo is May 5. Color it ▭▬▶ .

4. Color all Fridays in July ▭▬▶ .

Algebra Readiness ▶ Patterns

Use the May calendar above.
Write the dates for the Thursdays.

5. _____ _____ _____ _____ _____

6. **Talk About It** What pattern do you see?

Now write the dates for the Saturdays.

7. _____ _____ _____ _____ _____

8. **Talk About It** Is the pattern the same? Why?

At Home Help your child find your family's special days on a calendar.

Name _____

Use a Table

 Audio Tutor 2/4 Listen and Understand

Objective
Use information in a table to solve problems about elapsed time.

Use a table to get information.

The Wilsons are having a family picnic.

Dan picks up his family at the airport. Does Aunt Nora arrive before or after Grandma?

Use the table to solve.

Think
Find the times in the table.

Arrival Schedule

Person	Time
Grandma	12:00
Aunt Nora	3:00
Cousin Eva	6:00
Uncle Joe	8:00

Grandma arrives at __12:00__.

Aunt Nora arrives at __3:00__.

Aunt Nora arrives __after__ Grandma.

Use a table to help you solve problems.

Molly picks up Cousin Eva at the airport. How many hours will they have to wait to pick up Uncle Joe?

Use the table to solve.

Think
Find the first time in the table. Count on to get to the second time.

Cousin Eva arrives at ____:____.

Uncle Joe arrives at ____:____.

They wait for ____ hours.

Use the table to solve the problem.

Friday Schedule	
Activity	**Time**
Sign in	8:00
Boat trip	9:00
Lunch	12:00
Soccer game	2:00
Dinner	6:00

1. Cathy signs in at **8:00**. How much time does she have until the boat trip begins?

Think
Count on from 8:00 to 9:00 to find how much time until the boat trip.

Draw or write to explain.

_____

2. What activity starts **3** hours after the boat trip?

Think
Start at 9:00 and count on 3 hours.

_____

Practice

3. What activity begins **2** hours after lunch starts?

_____

4. How many hours are there between lunch and dinner?

_____ hours

Go on ➡

Name_____

Mixed Problem Solving

Strategies
Write a Number Sentence
Act It Out With Models
Draw a Picture

Solve.

Draw or write to explain.

1. Five children travel by train. Four adults travel with them. How many people travel on the train?

train

_____ people

2. Ten people travel by bus. Six people travel by car. How many more people travel by bus than by car?

bus

_____ more people

3. The Dunns and Hales travel by airplane. The Hales arrive at **2:00**. The Dunns arrive **3** hours later. What time do the Dunns arrive?

airplane

____ : ____

4. **Multistep** Sue's aunt arrives before her uncle. Her cousin arrives after her uncle and before her brother. Who arrives second?

car

_____

Chapter 13

At Home Make a schedule with your child showing his or her activities for one day.

three hundred eighty-one **381**

Problem Solving on Tests • Listening Skills

Carmela's Camp Schedule

Activity	Time
Swimming	8:00
Bike ride	10:00
Lunch	12:00
Soccer game	3:00
Dinner	6:00

Listen to your teacher read the problem. Solve.

Show your work using pictures, numbers, or words.

1. Carmela goes swimming at 8:00. How many hours does she have until the bike ride begins?

_____ hours

2. An hour after dinner starts Carmela reads a book. What time does she start reading?

_____ : _____

Multiple Choice

Listen to your teacher read the problem. Choose the correct answer.

3. 10:00   11:00   12:00   1:00
    ○   ○   ○   ○

4. 4 hours   3 hours   2 hours   1 hour
    ○   ○   ○   ○

Education Place
See **eduplace.com/map**
for more Test-Taking Tips.

Name_____

Time is measured in different ways.
These pictures show activities that take
hours, days, and weeks.

hours

days

weeks

Think about the length of time.
Draw or write things that you do
that take that long.

  1. Hours

---

  2. Days

---

  3. Weeks

Social Studies Connection
Rice Festival

Rice is eaten all over the world. Louisiana holds a Rice Festival.

The Rice Festival is always in October.

Look at the calendar. In some years the Rice Festival starts on October 21 and ends the next day.

Circle the date the festival ends.

Put a triangle around the date that is **2** days before Friday, October 21.

October

Sun.	Mon.	Tues.	Wed.	Thurs.	Fri.	Sat.
						1
2	3	4	5	6	7	8
9	10	11	12	13	14	15
16	17	18	19	20	21	22
23	24	25	26	27	28	29
30	31					

WEEKLY WR READER eduplace.com/map

Plane Shapes

Read the sorting rule.
Circle the shapes that follow the rule.

1. Shapes with more than 2 sides   2. Round shapes

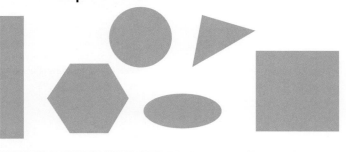 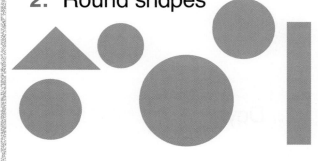

3. Write a sorting rule. _____

4. Circle all of the shapes that belong.

Extra Practice at **eduplace.com/map**

Chapter Review/Test

Vocabulary

Show 4 o'clock.

1. Draw the **minute hand**  .

2. Draw the **hour hand** 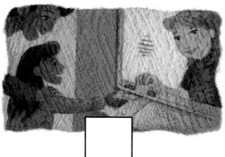 .

Concepts and Skills

Write 1, 2, and 3 to show the correct order.

3.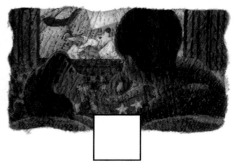

Circle the activity if it takes about 1 minute.
Draw an X on the activity if it takes more than 1 minute.

4.    5.    6.

Read the clock.
Write the time two ways.

7.

_____ o'clock

8.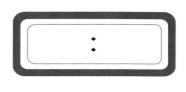

half past _____

Write how long the activity takes.

9.

Start  End

_____ hour

10.

Start  End

_____ hours

Show the time on the clock.

11. Math class starts at 10 o'clock.

[__ : __]

12. We play at half past 11.

13. How many Thursdays are in this month? _____

14. If yesterday was January 27, what is today's date?

_____

			January			
Sun.	Mon.	Tues.	Wed.	Thurs.	Fri.	Sat.
			1	2	3	4
5	6	7	8	9	10	11
12	13	14	15	16	17	18
19	20	21	22	23	24	25
26	27	28	29	30	31	

Problem Solving

Use the table to solve the problem.

15. Holly's dance class lasts 1 hour. What time does it end?

_____ : _____

Holly's Afternoon Schedule

Activity	Time
Dance	4:00
Homework	6:00
Bedtime	8:00

Using Money

INVESTIGATION

What items can she buy?

2¢

10¢

8¢

4¢

6¢

Selma Burke was born in Mooresville, North Carolina.

 # People Using Math

Selma Burke

Selma Burke was a sculptor, someone who shapes things out of clay. In 1940, she opened her own school to help others learn how to be sculptors.

In 1943, she won a contest to make a sculpture of President Franklin D. Roosevelt. Two years later, the sculpture was used as a model for his picture on the dime. The next time you have a dime, look at Selma Burke's art work.

Selma was **6** years old when she first made something out of clay.

1. How much money would she have, if she had **1** dime for each year of her age?

_____ ¢

2. How much money would you have, if you had **1** dime for each year of your age?

_____ ¢

Name _____

Value of Coins

 Audio Tutor 2/5 Listen and Understand

Objective
Identify coins and count groups of coins.

Vocabulary
penny   dime
nickel   cent

penny   **nickel**   **dime**

| cent   5 cents   10 cents

| ¢   5¢   10¢

Guided Practice

Use coins.
Find the value of the coins.

Think
The number I say last is the number of cents there are.

1. Count on by 1s to find the value of the pennies.

_____¢ _____¢ _____¢ _____¢ _____¢

_____¢

2. Count on by 5s to find the value of the nickels.

_____¢ _____¢ _____¢ _____¢ _____¢

_____¢

3. Count on by 10s to find the value of the dimes.

_____¢ _____¢ _____¢ _____¢

_____¢

Explain Your Thinking Name two ways to show 10¢.

Practice

Count on by
1s for pennies,
5s for nickels, and
10s for dimes.

Use coins.
Find the value of the coins.

1.

__1__¢ __2__¢ __3__¢ _____¢ _____¢ _____¢ _____¢   _____¢

2.

_____¢ _____¢ _____¢ _____¢   _____¢

3.

_____¢ _____¢ _____¢ _____¢ _____¢ _____¢ _____¢   _____¢

4.

_____¢ _____¢ _____¢ _____¢ _____¢ _____¢   _____¢

Problem Solving ▶ Reasoning

5. Grace has **10** pennies.
What coins can she
trade them for?

Draw or write to explain.

_____ dime or _____ nickels

 At Home Use pennies, nickels, or dimes. Make groups using one type
of coin totaling 40¢ or less. Have your child find the value of the group.

Name_____

Nickels and Pennies

Find the value of the coins.
Count the coin with the greater value first.

Objective
Find the value of a group of nickels and pennies.

Hands-On

> Count on by 5s for nickels.
> Count on by 1s for pennies.

___5___ ¢ ___10___ ¢ ___15___ ¢ ___16___ ¢ ___17___ ¢   ___17___ ¢

Guided Practice

Use coins.
Find the value of the coins.

Think
Count 5, 10, 15, 20, and then count on by 1s.

1.

   _____ ¢ _____ ¢ _____ ¢ _____ ¢ _____ ¢ _____ ¢   _____ ¢

2.

   _____ ¢ _____ ¢ _____ ¢ _____ ¢ _____ ¢ _____ ¢   _____ ¢

Explain Your Thinking Would you rather have 1 nickel or 4 pennies? Why?

Remember to count the coin with the greater value first.

Use coins.

Find the value of the coins.

1.

5 ¢   10 ¢   15 ¢   16 ¢   _____ ¢   _____ ¢

_____ ¢

2.

_____ ¢   _____ ¢   _____ ¢   _____ ¢   _____ ¢   _____ ¢

_____ ¢

3.

_____ ¢   _____ ¢   _____ ¢   _____ ¢   _____ ¢   _____ ¢

_____ ¢

4.

_____ ¢   _____ ¢   _____ ¢   _____ ¢   _____ ¢   _____ ¢

_____ ¢

Problem Solving ▸ Reasoning

5. Kevin has **2** nickels and **4** pennies.
Circle the top he can buy.

Draw or write to explain.

At Home Use nickels and pennies to make a group of coins that has a value less than 40¢. Have your child find the value of the coins. Repeat the activity using other amounts.

Name _____

Dimes and Pennies

Find the coins that match the price.
Count the coin with the greater value first.

Objective
Find the value of
a group of dimes
and pennies.

Hands-On

Count on by 10s for dimes.
Count on by 1s for pennies.

__10__ ¢ __20__ ¢ __21__ ¢ __22__ ¢ __23__ ¢

_23_ ¢

23¢

Guided Practice

Think
Count 10, 20,
30, and then count
on by 1s.

Use coins.
Find the value of the coins.

1.

_____¢ _____¢ _____¢ _____¢ _____¢ _____¢ _____¢   _____¢

Circle the coins that match the price.

2. **32¢**

Explain Your Thinking Look at Exercise 2. Does the
bigger coin have the greater value? Why?

Practice

Remember to count on by 10s for dimes and 1s for pennies.

Circle the coins that match the price.

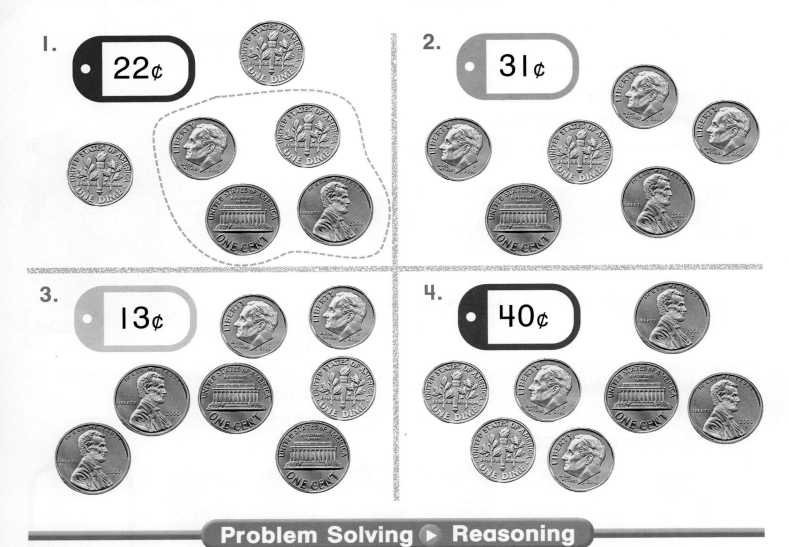

1. 22¢

2. 31¢

3. 13¢

4. 40¢

Problem Solving ▶ Reasoning

5. Each boy has 12¢.
These are Jason's coins.
Draw Ramon's coins.

Jason's

Ramon's

At Home Place 2 dimes and 5 pennies on a table.
394 three hundred ninety-four   Ask your child to show you 14¢ and 25¢.

Name_____

Count Coins

 Audio Tutor 2/6 Listen and Understand

Objective
Find the value of a group of dimes, nickels, and pennies.

Hands-On

Find the value of the coins.

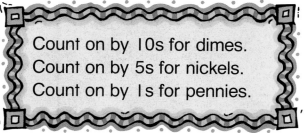
Count on by 10s for dimes.
Count on by 5s for nickels.
Count on by 1s for pennies.

__10__ ¢ __20__ ¢ __25__ ¢ __30__ ¢ __31__ ¢

__31__ ¢

Guided Practice

Think
Count the dimes first because they have the greater value.

Use coins.
Find the value of the coins.

1.

_____¢ _____¢ _____¢ _____¢ _____¢ _____¢

_____¢

2.

_____¢

Explain Your Thinking In Exercise 2 what coin did you start with and why?

Chapter 14 Lesson 4

Count the coin with the greatest value first.

Use coins.
Find the value of the coins.

1.  _40_ ¢

2. _____ ¢

3. _____ ¢

4. _____ ¢

Problem Solving ▶ Data Sense

5. Find the value of Rae's coins.

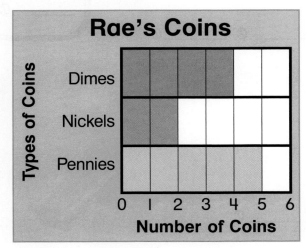

Rae's Coins

Types of Coins

Dimes
Nickels
Pennies

0 1 2 3 4 5 6
Number of Coins

Draw or write to explain.

_____ ¢

6. **Talk About It** Explain how you found your answer.

At Home Write 70¢. Have your child use coins to show that amount. Repeat the activity with other amounts.

Go on ➡

Activity

Name_____

Fun With Coins

2 Players

What You Need: paper clip, pencil, pennies, nickels, and dimes

How to Play

1. Take turns. Spin the spinner.

2. Take coins that match the coins where the spinner lands.

3. Trade pennies for nickels. Trade nickels for dimes.

4. Continue playing until a player has 60¢ with the fewest coins.

Other Ways to Play

A. Play without trading. The first player to have 60¢ with the most coins wins.

B. The first player to have 60¢ with only dimes and nickels wins.

Use coins.

Find the value of the coins.

1.

_____ ¢   _____ ¢   _____ ¢   _____ ¢   _____ ¢   _____ ¢   _____ ¢

2.

_____ ¢   _____ ¢   _____ ¢   _____ ¢   _____ ¢   _____ ¢   _____ ¢

3.

_____ ¢

4.

_____ ¢

Circle the coins that match the price.

5.    **31¢**   

Facts Practice, see page 675

Name_____

Quarters

quarter

25 cents

25¢

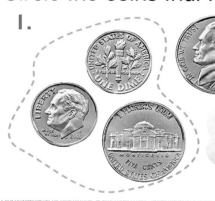

25¢

25¢

Guided Practice

Use coins.

Circle the coins that make 25¢.

1.

Think
I dime is 10¢
and I nickel is 5¢.

2.

3.

4.

Explain Your Thinking Can you make 25¢ with only dimes? Why or why not?

There are different ways to make **25¢**.
Use coins to help you complete the chart.

Make sure each row shows a different way to make 25¢.

5.	1	0	0	0
6.		2		
7.			0	5
8.				
9.				
10.				
11.				
12.				
13.				
14.				
15.				
16.				
17.				

Go on ➡

Count the coin with the greatest value first.

Circle the coins that match the price.

1. 45¢

2. 28¢

3. 35¢

4. 55¢

Problem Solving ▶ Reasoning

You can draw coins like this.

25¢ 5¢
10¢ 1¢

5. Show 22¢ with fewer coins.

Draw or write to explain.

At Home Find items under 50¢ in an advertisement. Have your child tell you the coins needed to buy each item.

You can use different coins to show
the same amount.

These coins show 21¢.

These coins show 21¢
another way.

Use coins.
Complete the chart.

Count these coins.	Write the amount.	Show another way.
1.	13 ¢	
2.	____ ¢	
3.	____ ¢	

Dollar

 Audio Tutor 2/7 Listen and Understand

Objective
Count groups of coins that equal one dollar.

one dollar

$1

100¢

one dollar bills   one dollar coins

A set of coins with a value of 100 cents equals one dollar.

25¢   50¢   75¢   100¢

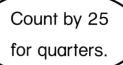

Count by 25 for quarters.

$ _____

Guided Practice

Find the value of the coins.

Think
You can skip count to find the answer.

1.

____¢ ____¢ ____¢ ____¢ ____¢

____¢ ____¢ ____¢ ____¢ ____¢

$____

2.

____¢ ____¢ ____¢ ____¢ ____¢ ____¢

$____

Explain Your Thinking Can you make one dollar with only pennies? How?

Practice

Find the value of the coins.

1.

$ _____

25 ¢   50 ¢   60 ¢   _____ ¢   _____ ¢   _____ ¢   _____ ¢

2.

_____ ¢   _____ ¢   _____ ¢   _____ ¢   _____ ¢   _____ ¢   _____ ¢

$ _____

_____ ¢   _____ ¢   _____ ¢   _____ ¢   _____ ¢   _____ ¢

Problem Solving ▶ Reasoning

3. Draw $1 using 4 coins.

4. Draw $1 using 8 coins.

404 four hundred four

At Home Ask your child to use coins and show one dollar in several different ways.

Name_____

Use a Picture

Objective
Recognize and use data from a picture to solve a problem.

10¢   20¢

30¢

30¢   10¢

30¢

10¢   15¢

At the yard sale, you can buy cars, marbles, and other toys.

Use the picture to help you decide how much money is needed.

Joey wants to buy a toy car.
He has **28**¢. What other coins does he need?

Think
Count on to find the amount he needs.

2 pennies
_____

Use the picture to help you decide how many can be bought.

Lita uses her money to buy marbles.
She has **2** dimes and **2** nickels.
How many marbles can she buy?

Think
First find the amount of money she has.

_____ marbles

Use coins and the picture to solve.

 40¢

 30¢

 32¢

1. Jared wants to buy the car. He has 1 dime. How many more dimes does he need?

Draw or write to explain.

Think
Count dimes by 10s.

_____ dimes

2. Ashley wants to use her nickels to buy the pen. How many nickels does she need?

Think
Count nickels by 5s.

_____ nickels

3. Chun wants to buy the ball. She has 28¢. What other coins does she need?

_____

4. Leon has 1 quarter, 2 dimes, 3 nickels, and 2 pennies. What two items can he buy?

_____ and _____

Go on

Name_____

Mixed Problem Solving

Strategies
Act It Out With Models
Draw a Picture
Write a Number Sentence

Use coins to solve.

Draw or write to explain.

1. Ethan has **2** coins. He has enough money to buy the whistle. What **2** coins does Ethan have?

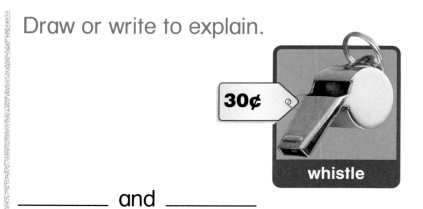
30¢ whistle

_____ and _____

2. Megan has **2** coins. One of her coins is a quarter. Can she buy the drum?

80¢ drum

_____

3. Rosa has **20**¢. Her dad gives her **10**¢ more. Can she buy the recorder? Explain.

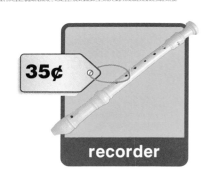
35¢ recorder

_____

4. Alex wants to buy the guitar. He has **5** dimes, **2** nickels, and **5** pennies. He finds **2** more pennies, but he loses **1** dime. How much money does he have now?

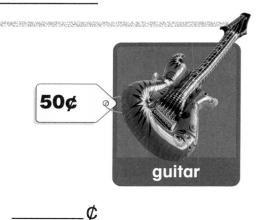
50¢ guitar

_____¢

At Home Ask your child to make up a money story problem using a picture from a magazine or a newspaper.

Problem Solving on Tests • Listening Skills

20¢

65¢

30¢

Listen to your teacher read the problem.
Solve.

1. Elena has 4 coins. She uses them to buy the notebook. What coins could she have?	Show your work using pictures, numbers, or words.
2. Alvin wants to buy the ruler and the pencil. He has 4 nickels. How many more nickels does he need?	_____ nickels

Listen to your teacher read the problem.
Choose the correct answer.

3.   2 pennies   3 pennies   4 pennies   5 pennies
           ○   ○   ○   ○

4.   5 dimes   6 dimes   7 dimes   8 dimes
           ○   ○   ○   ○

65¢

Education Place
See **eduplace.com/map**
for more Test-Taking Tips.

408 four hundred eight

Name_____

Now Try This $5, $10, $20

five dollar bills

ten dollar bills

twenty dollar bills

Match the bill to an equal amount.

1.

2.

3.

4. **Talk About It** What is another way to make
   $20 with one, five, and ten dollar bills?

Math Challenge
Coin Faces

Most faces on coins belong to U.S. presidents.
Match the coins and the clues.

F. Roosevelt — on the smallest coin
Washington — on the coin with the same value as 2 dimes and 1 nickel
Kennedy — on the largest coin
Lincoln — on the coin with the least value
Jefferson — on the coin with the same value as 5 pennies

Fractions

1. Draw a line to show halves.
Color $\frac{1}{2}$.

2. Draw lines to show fourths.
Color $\frac{1}{4}$.

3. Draw lines to show thirds.
Color $\frac{1}{3}$.

4. Color to show the fraction.

$\frac{1}{4}$

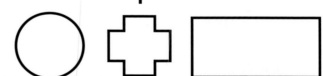

Extra Practice at **eduplace.com/map**

Name ______________________

Chapter Review/Test

Vocabulary

Match the coin or bill to its value.
Write the correct letter.

1. penny	______	a.	10¢
2. dime	______	b.	$1
3. quarter	______	c.	1¢
4. nickel	______	d.	25¢
5. one dollar	______	e.	5¢

Concepts and Skills

Find the value of the coins.

6.

______¢ ______¢ ______¢ ______¢ ______¢ ______¢ ______¢

Total: ______¢

7.

______¢ ______¢ ______¢ ______¢ ______¢ ______¢

Total: ______¢

8.

______¢ ______¢ ______¢ ______¢ ______¢ ______¢

Total: ______¢

9.

______¢ ______¢ ______¢ ______¢ ______¢ ______¢

Total: ______¢

Chapter Review/Test

Circle the coins that match the price.

10.  **28¢**

---

11.   **55¢**

---

12. Find the value of the coins.

_____¢   _____¢   _____¢   _____¢

$ _____

13.

_____¢ _____¢ _____¢ _____¢ _____¢ _____¢ _____¢

$ _____

Problem Solving

Use the picture to solve.

   25¢   **50¢**

Draw or write to explain.

14. Jed wants to buy the whistle. He has I dime. How many more dimes does he need?

_____ more dimes

---

15. Ann wants to use her nickels to buy the pen. How many nickels does she need?

_____ nickels

Half-Dollar

A half-dollar has the same value as two quarters.

It also has the same value as five dimes.

| half-dollar
50 cents
50¢ | two quarters
50 cents
50¢ | five dimes
50 cents
50¢ |

Find the value of the coins.

1.

_60_ ¢

2.

_____¢

3.

_____¢

4.

_____¢

Education Place
Visit **eduplace.com/map**
for brain teasers.

Computer
Money Matters

29¢

Use the coins and bills found at
eduplace.com/map.

I. Put your pointer over the
Stamp tool.
• Click the quarter.

2. Put your pointer over the
Stamp tool.
• Click the penny 4 times.

3. Click [I 2 3].

Use the coins and bills.
Show the amount using the fewest coins.

I.

32¢

2.

48¢

Vocabulary

Complete the sentence.

1. **25¢** is equal to **I** _____.

2. A _____ is **30** minutes long.

3. There are **60** seconds in **I** _____.

4. A _____ is equal to **5¢**.

> minute
>
> half-hour
>
> nickel
>
> quarter

Concepts and Skills

Read the clock.
Write the time two ways.

5.

_____ o'clock

6.

half past _____

Write how long the activity takes.

7.   **Start**   **End**

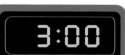

_____ hour

8.   **Start**   **End**

_____ hours

Find the value of the coins.

9.

_____ ¢

Unit 5 Test

Find the value of the coins.

10.

_____ ¢

Use the calendar to find the answer.

11. How many Tuesdays
are in this month? _____

12. What is the first
day of this month? _____

13. Color all Fridays ████▶ .

June

Sun.	Mon.	Tues.	Wed.	Thurs.	Fri.	Sat.
1	2	3	4	5	6	7
8	9	10	11	12	13	14
15	16	17	18	19	20	21
22	23	24	25	26	27	28
29	30					

Draw coins to show **32**¢ two different ways.

14.

Problem Solving
Solve.

15. Sue wants to buy the
yo-yo. She has **3** dimes
and **1** nickel. What other
coin does she need?

Draw or write to explain.

_____

Test-Taking Tips
· ·

Study the pictures carefully before you answer the question.

Check your work.

Multiple Choice

Fill in the ○ for the correct answer.

1. About how long does it take to snap your fingers 5 times?

less than a minute	1 minute
○	○

more than a minute	5 minutes
○	○

2. How many tens are there in 45?

0	2	4	5
○	○	○	○

3. What day of the week is July 4?

○ Thursday

○ Friday

○ Saturday

○ Sunday

July

Sun.	Mon.	Tues.	Wed.	Thurs.	Fri.	Sat.
		1	2	3	4	5
6	7	8	9	10	11	12
13	14	15	16	17	18	19
20	21	22	23	24	25	26
27	28	29	30	31		

4. What time is it?

1:00	2:30	7:00	7:10
○	○	○	○

Fill in the ○ for the correct answer.
N means Not Here.

Solve.

5. Mark how much in all.

7¢	8¢	15¢	17¢
○	○	○	○

6. What is the missing number?

20   25   30   ☐

21	25	35	N
○	○	○	○

7. Mark how much in all.

36¢	66¢	81¢	86¢
○	○	○	○

8. Read the clock.
Write the time two ways.

_____ : _____

_____ o'clock

9. Write a fraction to show what part of the kite has dots.

_____

10. What is the date of the second Tuesday in this month?

			May			
Sun.	Mon.	Tues.	Wed.	Thurs.	Fri.	Sat.
				1	2	3
4	5	6	7	8	9	10
11	12	13	14	15	16	17
18	19	20	21	22	23	24
25	26	27	28	29	30	31

Education Place

Look for Cumulative Test Prep at
eduplace.com/map for more practice.

A Walk Around the Farm

written by Margaret Lena
illustrated by C.D. Hullinger

READING MATH

Farm Family

Look back at the story to answer these questions.

● 1. Look at page 3. Two more lambs come to play. Add to find how many there are in all.

● 2. Look at page 5. If 2 ducklings fly away, how many would be left? Subtract.

▲ 3. Look at page 6. Add to find how many children and kittens there are in all.

★ 4. Make up a number story about other animals you might see on a farm.

Answers
1. $8 + 2 = 10$ 2. $9 - 2 = 7$ 3. $2 + 6 = 8$
4. Answers may vary.

Reading Strategies

● Cause and Effect   ▲ Noting Details   ★ Summarize

We stroll with Grandpa arm in arm,

To take a walk around the farm.

In the pigsty, 4 piglets squeal,

While 3 others wait for their meal.

How many piglets are there in all?

4 piglets + 3 piglets = ▨ piglets

Now our morning walk is done.

Seeing the animals was lots of fun!

Thank you, Grandpa, thanks a bunch.

Now we're hungry for some lunch!

How many children are ready for lunch?

1 child + 1 child = ▨ children

Mother sheep watch and guard

Their little lambs in the yard.

3 little lambs are fast asleep,

While 5 woolly lambs play and leap.

How many lambs are in the yard?

3 lambs + 5 lambs = ▢ lambs

In the barn and behind the plow,

We hear the sound of a cat's meow.

We see 6 kittens near the door.

Then 4 go off to explore.

How many kittens stay in the barn?

6 kittens – 4 kittens = ▢ kittens

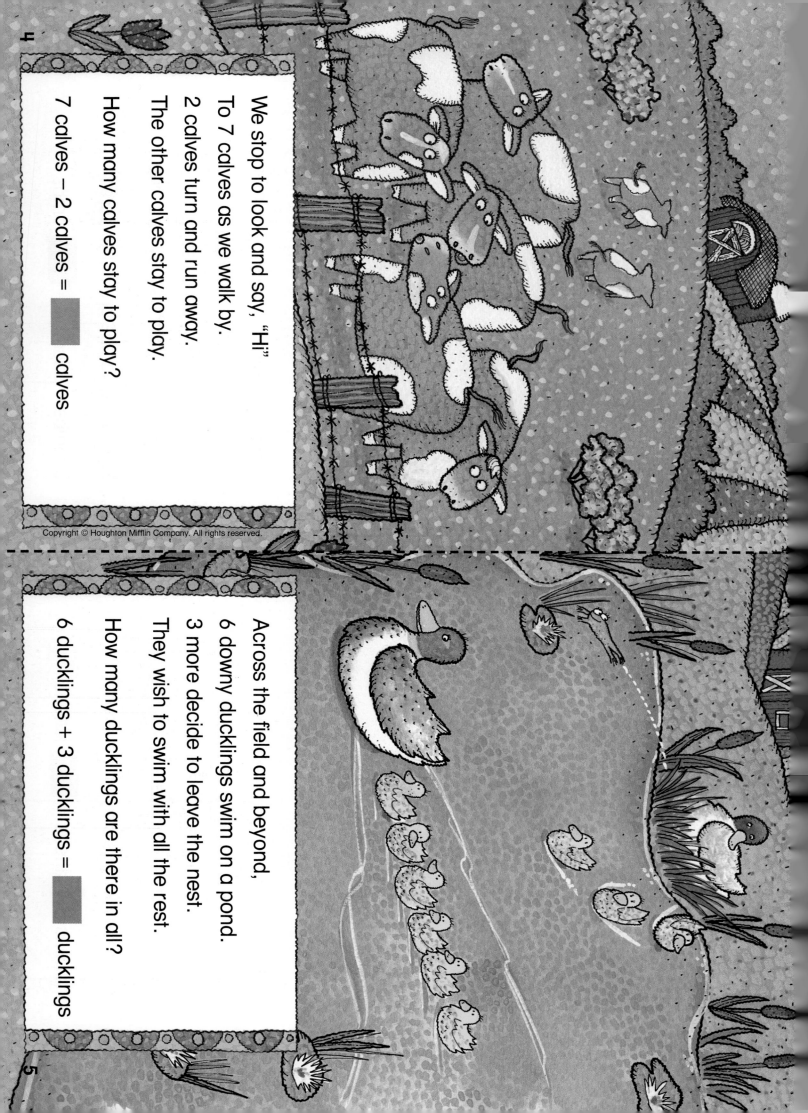

We stop to look and say, "Hi"
To 7 calves as we walk by.
2 calves turn and run away.
The other calves stay to play.

How many calves stay to play?

7 calves – 2 calves = ▢ calves

4

Across the field and beyond,
6 downy ducklings swim on a pond.
3 more decide to leave the nest.
They wish to swim with all the rest.

How many ducklings are there in all?

6 ducklings + 3 ducklings = ▢ ducklings

5